Orgasms, American Slavery and God

By

Larry A. Yff

SECTIONS

Introduction 3

1. Section One: Orgasms...and God

    ➤ Lesson One 4

    ➤ Lesson Two 7

    ➤ Lesson Three 13

2. Section Two: American Slavery...and God

    ➤ Lesson One 24

    ➤ Lesson Two 28

    ➤ Lesson Three 35

3. Lessons Summary with 5 essays on sex, slavery, niggas and cusswords. 43

INTRODUCTION

Sex provides the single-most, beautifullest, natural high found on the planet. American Slavery is one of the ugliest things that existed on the planet. God put both of them into the most genius, beautiful plan on the planet. This book ties them all together for you. Now remember, I live my life as close as I can to the Holy Bible standards, so that is where my view comes from. Our views may differ, but in the end your view matters and so does mine.

ORGASMS...and GOD

Lesson One

"Oh God! I'm about to cum!!!" Sound familiar? Orgasms are a beautiful, powerful thing. They are so powerful that a non-religious person will invoke the name of God when it comes to nothing else *except* for an orgasm, bustin'a nut, climaxing or whatever term you use for the endgame. Lesson One breaks down this all too familiar saying.

Let's start with "Oh God!" What is it about an orgasm that makes a person say this? I believe it has to do with part of our God-given purpose. The book of Genesis records an event where God told Adam and Eve to, "...multiply and fill the Earth with humans..." as part of our purpose here. How does that happen? With sex of course.

So my theory is whenever a person is about to have an orgasm or is in the middle of having one and mentions God, it is some sort of subconscious acknowledgement that the act fulfilled a primal urge as well as recognizing the spiritual aspect of it.

"I'm coming!" or "I'm about to cum" is the last part of the phrase we will take a look at. If you don't think about it, that part makes absolutely no sense. On the other hand, if you *do* think about it, it makes perfect sense.

When a person is going somewhere, or about to go somewhere, he or she will say, "I'm coming" or "I'm about to come." To say this during the act of sex implies there is something about the orgasm aspect of it that ties the orgasm to that person's soul kind of.

Once again: at first glance it makes no sense; but when you think about it, it does. "I" am made up of a physical body and some sort of unseen or spiritual element. When I'm having sex and say, "...I'm about to cum!" it does not mean I am about to come to your house for a bbq or that I'm on my way to meet you at the club. It means, from a man's perspective, that the physical part of me (my seed) and the spiritual part of me (my life-giving *soul* element that is somehow in my seed) are both on their way out. They are leaving one place and are about to come to another place.

And that is my way of tying "Oh God! I'm coming!!!" to our God: it acknowledges God's plan for sex.

Lesson Two

I believe God created the Universe. You may not agree with that statement, but at worst you *have* to admit humans did not make it. The part about the creation story Lesson Two focuses on is anatomy.

Since I believe God created the Universe, that includes humans and there are two natural species called males or females. (Let me add that there are humans who have been born with both male and female parts, but that is by far the exception and unnatural...*not* unimportant or irrelevant...just unnatural.)

The males have a penis (that I will be referring to as a dick), two testacles (that I will be referring to as balls), sperm/seed and testosterone; while the females have a vagina (that I will be referring to as a va-jay-jay), two breasts (that I will be referring to as titties), eggs, estrogen, uterus and hips that sway sexily from side to side.

Let's take a look at how the male and female body parts and chemical makeup are specifically designed to fit human's purpose in the reproductive part of God's plan.

A man has a dick. At the base of the dick are two balls that carry a man's sperm/seed. That sperm/seed carries two things: a man's DNA and I believe, some sort of spiritual element. I say that because when sperm and egg get together they create a human with a soul. Where that soul comes from I am not sure, but my view is it is somehow connected to the sperm/seed. I am not a dick-doctor and don't claim to be any type of spiritual or sex expert on that matter. Just remember I am simply sharing my view on orgasms...and God.

A dick sticks out and is designed to go in a hole. A female has a hole that typically is the right fit for your everyday, run-of-the-mill dick. That hole is called a va-jay-jay. In order for a human to be created naturally, a man must put his dick into a woman's va-jay-jay to the point of orgasm when his sperm/seed are released. These sperm/seeds go through the va-jay-jay and into the uterus where the woman has her eggs. Without being too technical, they say a man releases hundreds of thousands of sperm/seed into the uterus during an orgasm; but only one actually survives and is able to fertilize the egg. We are each literally a one-in-a-million, unique individual!

The uterus is designed to feed, nurture, develop, house and sustain a human from the embryo stage until birth. Those swaying hips females have aren't just to catch a man's attention: they expand. The female hips have that curvy shape to them because when it is time for the baby to be born, the hips (and/or cervix) naturally expand to allow the opening to accommodate the size of the baby that will be coming through there into the world.

While the baby is inside the uterus it is fed through an umbilical cord. Once the baby is born and they cut the cord, that in essence is cutting off the baby's original food source. That's where the titties come into play: they are not just fun-bags. Titties naturally produce milk. This milk has all the essential food groups and vitamins a baby needs to grow and develop properly.

The last part of the human design that is geared towards God's purpose of reproduction is chemical. Men have testosterone and females have estrogen. Testosterone in a man serves many purposes, but the one we are focusing on is sex-related. Testosterone makes you aggressive. It makes you want to tear shit up and be forceful.

Like we mentioned earlier: a man has a dick and in order to reproduce he needs to put that dick in a hole. The act of *putting, poking, sticking or placing* something somewhere is basically an aggressive act or motion. Since the goal of the dick is to get inside the va-jay-jay to shoot the owner's DNA-filled sperm/seed into the female's uterus and produce a child...he needs to have at least a natural, basic level of aggressiveness in his body in order to achieve that goal. Common-sense and any female will tell you, a man needs to get a little aggressive in order to get the job done of passing on the couple's DNA. A dick that is not supported with testosterone boosters would be unproductive when it comes to reproduction.

On the flip-side, the female has a natural chemical called estrogen. This chemical is typically not aggressive in its natural state; however...there are periods of time in a female's life where estrogen will bring female aggression to a whole new level that a man cannot match! Lucky for all the men in the world, this state of female aggression is pretty much limited to once a month or when a woman's child is put in any type of danger. Carrying on...

We are designed to reproduce. When God tells us to do something He already has available somewhere within your reach everything you need to get the job done. Going on a bunny trail (hopping to another subject), when God through the Bible says homosexual activity is a sin and is wrong, it's my view that 1) He said that because that type of sexual activity does not get the job done of reproduction that He designed the human body to do and 2) He allows some people to be drawn to that type of activity (naturally at times) for many reasons; one of which I believe is to show people what a sex life looks like the way He designed it and what a sex life looks like when His laws of sexual activity are not followed.

And that is my way of tying human anatomy to God: it acknowledges and supports God's plan of reproduction through having an orgasm.

Lesson Three

A sex conversation without talking about porno's and strip clubs would be incomplete...so we're gonna talk about them. A little background on me. I had an addiction to pornos (which I will be referring to as flicks) and I guess you would call it an addiction to strip clubs.

I had children at an early and immature time in my life. At one point I didn't think any female would want to be with that type of man: sexually irresponsible with kids by different women. At the same time, my natural drive for sex didn't leave.

Feeling that a real sex life was out of my grasp, I chose to opt for the sexual fantasy life. For me this was not just flicks and stripper-sex...it included drugs. My drug of choice was cocaine. It gave me an unnatural, heightened sense of sexual pleasure as well as numbed my sexual compass to the point where sex and orgasms were all that mattered. Visual stimulation outweighed any kind of thoughts about having a family, raising kids and eventually enjoying life with the grandkids.

I could go into the whole spiel about how Satan knows God's plan for human sexuality and wants to make a mockery of it and uses flicks and strip-clubs to achieve it…but I won't. I will simply say that the presence and high-availability of the sex-market *definitely* goes against God's plan for humanity in my view.

Meeting a soul-mate, lover, life-partner, potential husband or wife is a natural drive towards fulfilling one's purpose in life. Hooking up with strippers, using sex drugs and watching flicks is the unnatural, substitute way to fulfill one's sex life.

I would go to strip clubs for the fantasy of it all. I knew the stripper didn't love me. I knew she didn't give a shit about how my day was and I also knew any interest she did show towards me would end as soon as the process of me going in my pocket and grabbing more money for her ended. But I didn't care.

That natural drive I had for some type of sexual experience outweighed any thoughts of having a normal relationship. I was lost. I just wanted the thrill, the fantasy and the short-term satisfaction of being wanted sexually *even* if it meant I had to pay for it with money or drugs. The deeper I got into flicks, strippers and drugs, the further away I got from being able to use my sexuality for God's true purpose in my life.

In fact, I didn't care about God's plan for my sex life. I had gotten to the point where I viewed sex as a means to an end. In other words, I was content to enjoy the rush of taking a hit from my pipe (crack pipe) or sniffing a line of blow (cocaine)...waiting for the chemicals to reach my brain and give me an endorphin rush and stimulate my body sexually. That same endorphin rush is released from natural activities such as sex, laughing, eating certain foods and exercise.

As I allowed myself to get lost in sexual fantasy land, I began to experience depression. Major depression. At first the depression stemmed from purely physical reasons. After a night of chasing a sexual high through drug use, I would find myself hating myself the next day for going down that road again. It made me feel like a fraud and a fake. Here I was with a sex drive that could only be fulfilled through drugs, fantasies and money.

For me, it got so bad, I could easily leave the house for a store run and not return for two days. During those two days it wasn't uncommon for me to spend hundreds of dollars on blow or crack and spend hundreds of minutes staring intently at the television or my phone. You see, I had a dual-excitement level in my fantasy life. The minute I knew I was about to get high, I would get the porn website on my phone loaded and ready for viewing or I would start searching through the television for music videos or any other type of programming that had images of sexxxy females. I could do the whole get-high period without bathing, eating or drinking: all I wanted to feel was the rush of the drug, the visual stimulation from whatever I was watching and either physically pleasuring myself or getting assistance from some female who *enjoyed* the same activity I was *enjoying.*

I would be depressed because I knew there was some sort of natural endgame for my sexual desires and I just couldn't put my hand on 'em no matter how many times I tried with the route I was on. The depression was getting deeper, but not deep enough to make me want to stop. The addiction aspect of my fantasy sex life had a tight ass-grip on me and wasn't planning on letting go any time soon. The financial cost of the get-high situation was irrelevant to me.

Eventually I began to get back into the church. This had very little if any positive effect on my dismal situation. I would look around at all the smiling faces in church and wonder who in there had a problem with pornos or alcohol that was living in a state of denial for the sake of looking good on Sunday. I felt out of place in the church. I began to wonder why if I was the only person in the congregation to go through what I was going through and if so...the church was no place for me. If there was nobody who had experienced my level of shame and hopelessness, there would be nobody for me to reach out to and get physical or spiritual help.

The positive changes began when I shifted from focusing on the physical and human aspects of the church and began to focus on the scriptural basis for religion. I now was focused on understanding who God was, who Jesus was, who the Holy Spirit was and how could I find the same joy the rest of the church had in knowing these three, important beings. The crazy thing was that my positive change came not from what I was learning about sex...it was from learning about how much God loved me. As I began to see the rationale in His planning for the Earth through natural laws and how His laws for the world He created make a ton of sense, I began to put God to the test. I will only talk about the first way I began to test God to spare you the details of all the various things I did that in the end proved to be the source of my deliverance from addictions and on track to a successful life.

Tithing. The Bible teaches us about tithing. It's basically a taxing or membership type of transaction. For instance, if you support gun laws you give money to support the NRA and other organizations. Your display of giving lets people know what you believe in and that you are supporting that organization financially so it can continue to deliver its' agenda. Another good example for how tithing works it taxes. If you live in the United States of America, you pay federal, state, local, sales, personal and business tax based on the level of income you generated. Since you generated income or made a living from the system that is responsible for your safety (military), builds roads that you travelled on to and from work, provides police, fire and ambulance services to you and a host of other services that are paid for with tax dollars, the act of paying back into that system with your tax dollars shows you support it, believe in it and want that system to continue to deliver its' agenda of providing goods and services for its' citizens.

I chose tithing because that was the one area that God specifically asked us to test Him. In Malachi 3 He literally says, "…bring the full tithe to My house and see if I don't provide you with so many blessings and wealth that you won't be able to handle it all…" I did a little more research on tithing because pastors always say, "…pay your tithes because if you don't, you are literally stealing from God!!" God led me to take a look at Malachi 1. In this book I found out the true meaning of what "stealing from God" was all about. It had nothing to do with paying money to the church and it had *everything* to do with giving God respect and honor for creating this magnificent world we live in.

It was like the tax example: In Malachi 1 God says, "…you give honor and respect to everyone but me. Where is the honor and respect you owe me???" That verse opened my eyes to the most major, Biblical, historically accurate information that made me proactive in my life! I knew humans didn't make this Earth. I believed God made it everything in existence. I believed God had excellent planning for life as we know it (the Earth is the only planet with an ozone layer, water, plant life, bees for pollination, etc.) and when I was getting high as shit I wasn't giving Him respect or honor! Tithing was my way of starting to right my wrongs and pay into the system He created; thus giving Him the honor and respect He deserves.

    I would still get high, but now it wouldn't be a depression from how much money I had jacked off or how I was allowing my dope boy and the females to take advantage of me and my money…it was a depression from the realization that I was literally stealing from God, the being who gave me this wonderful opportunity called life and I was wasting it. Like I said, my addiction didn't leave me right away. The first difference was I began to get paid and send my tithe money off to the church immediately. That way, in the most likely event I would get high at least I would give God His respect through my tithing.

That recognition of how my finances are supposed to be used turned the tide. Since I was paying into a system, I started too long to receive the benefits of it. I wanted to be happy in life. I wanted to be a better dad, son and uncle. I wanted to have a meaningful career and I even, for the first time, wanted to begin to have a normal sex life with a real female who really loved me and *maybe, possibly, potentially* get married!

To make a long ass story just a tad bit shorter, all the lusting, the pornos, strip clubs, drug use, all of it began to get on my nerves and make me sick. That activity began to actually anger me. I was angry because those activities helped keep me from a real relationship with my creator and I allowed every stupid ass, dumb ass, drug-filled, mutha fuckin' second of it to happen! Part of my purpose now is to expose the realities of a life of fantasy and introduce people to the benefits and blessings of a life of reality in God.

And that is my way of tying pornos, drugs and strip clubs to God: you will never find long-lasting happiness, confusion-free enjoyment or fulfillment in any type of sexual lifestyle that does not fit God's plan for human sexuality. That's my view and also that's the end of the "Orgasms and God" section. The next section is about American Slavery and God.

American Slavery...and GOD

Lesson One

"After I fuck her and some of my white male visitors fuck her *then* you can marry her" said the white, male slave master to his black male slave who asked, as was the "law" down south during slavery, for permission from his slave master to marry the woman of his dreams...while the slave master's white wife said nothing.

"Take that nigger and cut his dick off, burn him alive and hang him from the tallest tree you find" said the group of white males in regards to hanging a young black male suspected of looking at a white girl...while the all white crowd of journalists and white families with children all silently watched and recorded the incident without objection.

"That's a good looking slave family right there. I'll buy them all. I will then sell the black couple's daughters to a slave owner in Georgia I know...all except one. She's cute and young and I will rape her and make her my sex slave and *then* sell her. I will keep their sons as my slaves. The dad is a little old so I will make a profit off him by selling him to some local slave owner and I know a slave owner in Mississippi who needed a black bitch like the mama here to mate with. He's low on slave stock but he has some good breeding male slaves who will produce strong stock with her." This was all said by the white, male slave master while the black slave family was being parceled up in front of each other's eyes crying hysterically from the trauma of the situation...while the eyes of the white wife of the slave master were dry as she remained silent.

There are very few things I could say on the topic of slavery that are positive. In fact, there is literally only one thing I can say that was positive and that is: I believe American Slavery was able to be a part of God's plan just like everything else that happens here on Earth. It may seem like a stretch, especially coming from a black, African American male...but hear me out.

What if slavery never happened? America and the world would not be the way it is without the contributions and presence of a unique cultural group called African Americans. Like it or not, American Slavery is the institution that shaped America and helped America have the worldly influence it has today.

Let's be real about this though: there was *nothing* voluntary about African American's contributions to society since its inception. It's not like America was on the African's "Top Five Vacation Spots" list. Africans were probably like, "Fuck America. We got our own system here with kings, queens, governments, currency, universities, armies and societies like every other country. Why in the fuck would we want to give up this to go to America as slaves?" Once again, we have to be very clear about this: the despicable thing called American Slavery was able to be used by God Himself to benefit the world as we know it.

Lesson Two

What would life be like without the "Mikes"? I'm talking about Mike Tyson, Michael Jackson, Michael K. Williams, Michael Clarke Duncan, Michael Ealy and Michael Jordan. Some of you, and I can go so far as saying the *you* is primarily African Americans, may not like the fact that I am first mentioning sports and entertainment as one of the major ways African Americans have changed the world. This stems from the way black people were treated in these areas.

The white-male controlled media had black actors, but they played all the shitty parts like the nanny, the slave, the butler...all the lowest positions in society. White people hated black people so much that it was often times a white person *playing* the role of a black person; typically this white person had his or her face painted jet black as a direct mockery of black people. Once again, these black-face roles were primarily played by white males...while the white women remained silent. You will notice I make a point of adding, "...by the white males..." or "...while the white woman remained silent..." The reason for that will be revealed in Lesson Three of this section.

Most black people would not see the beauty in those actor/actress scenarios at all. They would view it as a reminder of how cruel, ignorant and oblivious to humanity white people, led by the white male, in those days were. I'm sure there is also a large number of white people who look back in disgust at that sort of activity.

Here comes some of the beauty I told you I would share with you. America's negative view of black people way before modern media. White America showed the entire world what they thought about black people with American Slavery. They followed this up with horrible depictions in movies and television...but God. Actors such as Michael Clark Duncan,

Michael K. Williams, Michael Ealy and Michael Jai White were all able to reverse the stereotypes and negativity about black people that American Slavery and American media tried to portray. Their ability to portray African American life and acting talent is remarkable considering the thousands, if not millions, of negative displays by White America for hundreds of years. That feat in itself is huge and an excellent display of the strength and durability of humans, even in the face of such degradation, can stand strong.

How many people have been able to express themselves through the music of Michael Jackson??? I can't and I won't even attempt to talk about his impact on not only American society, but also the world at large. People cry, shake and pass out just from being able to touch his hand! There are thousands of stories from people who will swear Michael Jackson and his music saved their lives somehow. He showed the world what a human is capable when it comes to delivering a message through music and entertainment.

Mike Tyson might be a difficult one to defend on this list. This crazy mutha fucka made the list for violently beating the shit out of people…professionally of course. He made the list because the entire world of boxing was influenced by "Iron Mike" Tyson. He may have gone off the crazy deep end several times in his life; but to his credit, the same influence he had in the world of boxing he was able to have in the world of motivational speaking. "Iron Mike" now has a testimony he shares publicly that is spectacular. He is an excellent example of how a human can come from a violent world of crime and, with proper guidance, can dominate the arena of his or her talents.

Michael Jordan made the cut for obvious reasons. He was able to use his athleticism to turn the entire sport of basketball around. During one dunk contest he actually flew to the rim! Until he came, there were no multi-million dollar shoe deals.

There were no multi-million dollar sold out basketball games. There were no multi-billion dollar companies made from the sport of basketball. There was no massive class of sports recruiters generating billions of dollars in revenue signing up basketball players. Michael Jordan is an excellent example of how a human can, once again, if properly guided and groom, influence not only the arena of his athletic skill but influence millions of people in a positive way who couldn't make a layup if their lives depended on it.

 Here's the closing paragraphs for this lesson. All of the billions of dollars in revenue black athletes and entertainers generated, the millions of black people who were able to use sports as a positive way to live life and escape horrible surroundings and neighborhoods would not have been able to be the examples of the durability humans have in the face of tough odds if it wasn't for the contributions of white males.

The "collaboration" of white and black people was the *only* way these life-changing examples in humanity could have existed and American Slavery is what brought the two races together. A white man invented basketball. In the beginning it was boring as shit. Nobody was dunking or dressed fashionably. They wore booty-shorts and shot layups and free-throws the entire game. The revenue from the entire pre-black basketball era was *maybe* $200,000 and now because of all the wealth generated from that sport, that's the standard salary of an assistant coach on a professional basketball team. Basketball has brought white and black people together like few other areas in society can.

The boxing world was pretty bland too. Enter Joe Louis, Muhammad Ali, George Foreman and our "Mike" and now boxing is a multi-billion dollar sport with fans around the world crossing all racial lines. The world of entertainment, movies and television have united black and white people on a level pre-black America never could have, or wanted to, conceive as possible. Michael

Jackson used his talent to generate billions of dollars of wealth for both black and white people; uniting blacks and whites like never before in the pre-black music industry.

Do I believe a world where black and white people could live together in somewhat of a normalized state could have existed without slavery? Yeah. I believe that's possible BUT it didn't happen that way. Whether you like it or not, you have to acknowledge that American Slavery, with all its hate, evilness, raping, vileness and inhuman acts of one human to another wound up being the secret sauce for American society. Planned? I think so. I believe everything in life can be used or was designed to be used to fit into God's plan for humanity.

And that is my way of tying American Slavery to God: American Slavery in my view shows that there is no situation human's cannot survive and there is nothing God cannot use to display the awesomeness humans have within them. An awesomeness God designed each and every one of us with.

Lesson Three

I touched on my reference to "white males" a lot in Lesson Two and said I would explain why. There is a shit ton of hatred just under the surface in America that stems from slavery. Every white male is probably, literally one wrong statement away from getting his ass beat by a black male. Let me explain this.

American Slavery was a hideous form of control. It was the white man's tool to get a heads-up on the entire portion of Africans that were used as slaves; particularly the black males. Males by nature are territorial. We want to eliminate rival males and capture the prize: females. Females are the key to any male wanting to continue his bloodline. Remember, in my view, *all* humans were given this assignment from God and it's instilled in every man naturally.

Enter slavery. In order to profit off slavery, it was the white males who did the actual slave trading. It was the white males who were the actual slave masters. It was the white males who would take the black slave male's wife and rape her in front of him. It was the white males who made up the political class of America in its early stages and made slavery of blacks legal in America.

If you fast forward to post-slavery times, it was the white males who were the police officers responsible for 100% of the killing of black men, women and children, often times for no other reason than they were black, and never seeing a day of prison time for their "in the line of duty" murders. Do you know what the term "white flight" means? It's the process where white people, led by white males, hated the site of black families moving into white neighborhoods and would at first burn the black family's house down and beat the black children up as they walked to school...once again, without ever seeing a day in court for their actions.

Eventually "white flight" kicked in. White males took their families and moved out of the cities and urban areas to avoid having black neighbors. They took their businesses, property tax revenue and educational assets with them. These businesses included financial institutions like banks. These banks were used to fund *only* white business ventures and white entrepreneurs, who at this time were all white males. With no access to local capital, no economic growth was allowed to take place in the urban areas where black families began to move in.

Black men were unable to support their families with legal jobs (they were denied any type of meaningful promotion by their white managers and supervisors) and had to resort to illegal means just to survive. Eventually drugs were introduced into the urban areas by white men who had access to drug importing and exporting either through government agencies run by white males such as the CIA or through other personal means.

As generations of black men turned to this lucrative means of income, inner-city turf wars began to build to protect their drug-dealing areas. This created black American gangs. Now America has generations of black males teaching their sons and raising them in the only conditions, neighborhoods and environments white, male government officials would allow. Take all that daily stress for generations upon the black male and then add the police department.

Local, white male police officers were instructed by the white males in the government to kill and eradicate any black males caught selling drugs. So now, white males have the government behind them to destroy black families by legally locking up and killing black males who, for generations, have been forced into illegal incomes to provide for themselves and their families.

I could go on and on but I won't. I hope I adequately painted the picture on the level of pure hatred black males have been ingrained to have towards anything white in America...particularly white males. Let's also be clear on this subject matter. It was not black males who just started hating white males. It was the result of the white males deliberate actions to wipe out and take advantage of their black male rivals that started the ball rolling.

I also want to point out that in my view, I cannot clearly say black males, if put in the same position as white males during the American Slavery era, would not have acted in the same territorial manner.

I would like to quickly tie in American Slavery to God's plan for our sexual purpose on Earth. In the Bible it says God basically old the man and the woman (Adam and Eve), "I created the man and woman to complement each other sexually. I did this so men and women can create human life through sex..." This purpose that I believe is instilled in every human regardless of skin color, is such a natural, driving force that even though black males were being attacked and killed from all angles (mostly systematically and intentionally from white-male run institutions), they still had the drive to have sex, create families and support them any way they could.

Let's circle back to the underlying hate that black males have towards white America...more specifically white males. With slavery being gone and more areas of society looking for cultural diversity answers to keep the peace, it is more relevant than ever, in my view, to focus on the Bible.

The Bible is based on historically accurate, eyewitness information about God. God has a track record of wanting to protect Earth and its' worldly system out of love. He went so far as to send His only Son Jesus to Earth to be the example on how we humans are to love one another NOT based on human laws that can be tainted with prejudice, bias, greed and hate; but on Bible laws from God that all have love, discipline and respect as their basis with no thoughts of greed, lust or financial gain as motivation.

If the World, and America in particular, is to ever eliminate, or at least begin to get over, the extreme hate and chaos white American males have generationally created and supported...a return to legislation and ensuing action based on God's laws is necessary. We already say, "In God we trust" in our court systems and on our currency. We already say, "God bless America" in our national anthem and at the end of every American political speech. Now it's time to apply God into our legislation and act on it according to the examples given in the Bible.

That's my view and the end of the "American Slavery...and God" section. In the end, myself, as a black male, do not hate all white males BUT it is hard as fuck when white-male run institutions act oblivious to any type of cultural responsibility to help right the wrongs of past generations. I have taken myself out of the black male vs white male arena by focusing on God's laws. His laws are positioning myself and others to begin to systematically take over every area of society that has been generationally tainted by prejudice and provide me (and us) with the financial resources to rebuild them based on laws that cross all color lines, social classes and religious/spiritual beliefs.

SUMMARY

Before you read the book I'm sure it was hard to imagine how sex, orgasms, slavery and Mike Tyson were all part of God's plan. Actually, *after* reading the book so far I'm sure it was hard to imagine how sex, orgasms, slavery and Mike Tyson were all part of God's plan. Either way it goes, I wanted to use this book as an example. It's an example on how to express your view in your words on any given subject.

It doesn't matter if we agree or not. In fact, if we were more willing to open up and share our views, we may find out that we have more in common with each other than we think. What you just read is my view. It's based on being an African American. It's based on my personal relationship with God as I understand Him to be from the Bible. It's based on me being adopted into a white family at one month old. It's based on my personal experiences and my view matters just like your view matters.

Following are the five essays I mentioned on some very important topics. These essays kind of narrow down my view on some issues that are related to the topics in this book. Typically it would be called the "Private Matters" section. That's because the things I talk about, and the words I use, are often done in private. I know a lot of religious people hate me saying fuck, shit or mutha fucka; while some people may be mad about me using the term nigga…but hey, that's how I talk in private sometimes with people close to me and in my view, I should have the right to express myself in my words in any setting the way I want to. Alright, enjoy the essays on the word nigga, slavery, sex and cuss words.

THE POSITIVE EFFECTS OF SLAVERY IN AMERICA

A Christian, African American Male's Perspective

Slavery at its core is not an equally beneficial process for both parties. People who lived through slavery in the United States have, and rightfully so, a stronger emotional connection and reaction to this issue than a student or observer of this topic. For my generation they were just that: stories. For the survivors and the first couple of generations after the "official end of slavery", the heinous stories we read in American history books were their realities and everyday nightmares. This Town Hall Topic discussion is to recognize the effects, positive and negative, that past generations of whites and blacks have had on making America what it is today from a Biblical perspective.

1. American slavery was inflicted upon African Americans by White Americans. True or false?
    - If you say true, is it fair to blame and judge the entire White race in America for slavery? If so, how accurate is that assessment?
    - If you say false, then is it a more accurate statement to say *some* Whites inflicted American slavery upon African Americans? One could even safely go so far as to say that the majority of White Americans at that time were directly or passively involved with the enforcement of American slavery.

2. I believe it is more accurate to say that *some* White Americans a couple of generations ago were absolutely guilty of supporting that system.
    - Is it the responsibility of the current generation of White Americans to fix it? If yes, what would a practical and implementable solution be?
    - If no, then who is responsible to correct past wrongs and what practical steps should be taken to hold the past generation responsible for their behavior?
3. How should Christians view and respond to these issues? What should our focus be? We should do what the Bible says and "seek first the Kingdom of God." This means look at how God acted in substantively similar scenarios in the Bible.
    - Is the Daniel[1] story a good example? In this story, Daniel and the majority of the Israelites were taken into slavery to a foreign country. The end result was that God used slavery as a means to establish His faithful ones to be Governors and visible examples of living a Godly life in the midst of national persecution on foreign soil.
    - Is the Joseph[2] story a good example? God allowed His faithful Joseph to be sold into slavery by his brothers. The end result was that God used slavery to elevate His faithful one to Ruler of the land and ultimately save that entire country and save the

---

[1] Daniel 1
[2] Genesis 37:26

Israelites from starving to death during a 7-year famine.
- Is the story of how God's chosen people, the Israelites, were allowed to remain as slaves in Egypt[3] for 400 years a good example? The end result was for God to raise up His faithful guy Moses as a very visible display of domination and leadership over the very powerful Egyptian Empire while giving glory to God.
- There is another story of the Israelites being slaves and lived on the outskirts in their own little cities and God instructed them to marry and work with them.

4. What does this tell us we should expect?
  - In the Bible, the people taken into slavery ultimately were part of a bigger plan. Is it possible that God used American slavery as a way to raise up His faithful ones in a country that has the resources that those individuals need to operate in to glorify God in front of the whole world?
  - America has become the most financially rich country in the world. God needs someone He can trust to control and disperse all this collected wealth properly.
  - America has the most powerful military system in the world. God needs someone that He can trust to control this military and use it in a way to protect America AND be the force to protect and

---

[3] Exodus 1:11

serve the unprotected and unserved around the World.
- America has a political system that when properly used gives EVERY person a voice and allows laws to be amended and officials elected peacefully. God needs someone in charge of this system that He can trust to make sure this system does what it's designed to do: protect His "garden" and subdue it. America's political system has been a dominating force in shaping World policies.

5. **Conclusion:** When you focus on the problem the solution doesn't get the attention it needs. When you focus on payback you can't pay it forward. America is only in this position because of the contributions of every cultural group that is and that has ever been here. If you were to take away or discredit the contributions of any cultural group, America's position drops drastically. The most practical way to correct the past is by correcting your mentality.

6. **Solutions:**
    - Think for yourself: If you form your views based on what your cultural group does or should be…you are limiting your personal development and growth in every area of your life and you can be easily swayed, played and manipulated. Look at the shift in dollars that sports generate in America once players played based on skill level instead of cultural group. That shift has created wealth and influence that would never have been reached if sports stayed the way they were pre

1970 or so. Politics, business and entertainment also all benefitted drastically as a result of breaking down cultural barriers.

- Focus on getting yourself in the position where God can put you on the mountaintop and use you. Focus on aligning yourself with other people interested in that. Focus on finding those "diamonds in the rough" that have been overlooked who can help your and God's cause.
- Keep problems in perspective: If a white cop kills a black kid…that simply means a specific white cop killed a specific black kid. It does not mean the entire police force in that city is corrupt. It does not mean black lives don't matter. How comfortable would you feel carrying a sign saying "white lives matter"? That's all a distraction to get people to operate only along cultural lines; while the REAL problem never gets addressed. The real problem is: these shootings primarily happen in areas where residents are not exposed and don't have access to the necessary resources (mentoring, correct spiritual teaching, financial, job opportunities) to make their communities places where there is no need for strong police presence.
- Consistently support a local mentoring program with your time or money. Consistently support local agencies that actively help residents become employable AND connect them to employers on a regular basis. You and some friends create

support groups for young people or single parents or whatever you have a passion for.
- Consistently make choices that allow you to do your passion and be the best Christian/person you can be. Your life choices determine your level of usefulness in Kingdom work AND your passion and purpose in life. You may not have money to support a local cause because you spend it partying on the weekends. You may make sexual choices that go against the Bible and now you find yourself a single parent feeling like you HAVE to work two jobs and hustle and you deserve to party on the weekend as an escape. We have shifted our focus to "Nobody can judge me because I'm taking care of me and my kids and working two jobs and paying my rent and car note" and there is rightfully a sense of pride in that; but what would happen if we focused on saying "I've been making choices that are from the Bible and I've been able to have a car and a house and a job and help other people?"

MY NIGGA

People say I belong to the cultural group called either Black or African American or Afro American or Negro. Members of this (or technically "these") cultural groups have their own rationale for why they prefer the term they chose. What's the importance of finding the politically correct term at all? And how does the word "nigga" fit into this picture?

Here's how. Humans love to be a part of something. It doesn't matter what cultural or religious group you are in, you want to be a part of something. Kids shoot up their schools as a result of not fitting in. Politicians vote against common sense just to fit in with their political party. Police officers remain silent while their fellow co-workers inflict harm on the people they are sworn to protect because they want to remain part of the police union. It's human nature.

When Africans came to the United States through the slave trade, white people who were linked to the slave trade here were taught how to get the best "results" and compliance from their slaves. All of the methods that were taught, and then consequently passed down through the generations, dealt with isolation.

The African slaves constantly had their lives and families forcibly and intentionally disrupted and kept in a constant state of fear. This was backed up by the Constitution of the United States as well as the majority of courthouse rulings in America. State, Federal and Local law enforcement also routinely used violence, often times lethal violence, to "legally" keep up this disruptive practice and state of confusion.

Common tactics were to have the kids of slave couples being sold off to different plantations. They were forced to not use their native African languages. They weren't allowed to learn how to read English. Everything that was inflicted on black people was intentionally and deceptively designed to not let them unite as a cultural group. Being part of a cultural group is a symbol of humanity. In order for white America to continue to benefit from slave activity, black people had to be denied a specific, legitimate cultural identity...forcing them into sub-human status in American society.

And this is where the word "nigga" fits in. Regardless to your complexion (light or dark), you were considered to be a nigga. White Americans began with legitimate terms from other languages that meant black such as negro and niger. In the end, they settled for the term nigga and nigger.

And there it is: Africans that were transplanted to America as slaves suddenly found themselves with a name that was recognized, used and identified them as a group no matter where they went in America. They were now officially nigga's or nigger's.

As is typical with human nature, black people now began to identify themselves and other members of this new "cultural group" by nigga. It began to take on an eerie, yet affectionate, tone. This was the underlying result of belonging. Black people now "belonged" in America as a "legitimate" cultural group.

The problem is that black people had this term forced on them. In the eyes of most white people and the courts, this term represented everything negative about humanity. It was bad enough that blacks had to start off legally in American society as sub-humans. They now had to carry this label with them and somehow make it work. They made it work too good.

The passion, the closeness, the pain of being labeled a curse yet feeling like a blessing, the genuine familial bonds that were forged behind this word all made it seem attractive. The realness of the need to want to be a part of something to the point where you take on the worst possible label and surviving is captivating. Making it through the legal challenges and persecutions, rapings, lynchings and beatings showed a resilience that people want to identify with. This mental fortitude and strength of black Americans, just like the generational frame of mind that white Americans passed onto their children, was as legitimate as any other culture's passing of generational ways.

Black people who use the word nigga use it and accept the good and bad elements of it without shame.

White people who use the word nigga either use it because of the magnetism of its realness or as a pitiful expression of racism that has no sting, trauma-tied experience or generationally taught power over people of this generation or the previous one...or future one's.

It is my opinion that real seeks real. Unity seeks unity. Human bonding is universal. If using the word nigga feels right in your soul...use it. If it doesn't...then don't. Anyone who uses this term that is not black must use it "responsibly". That means they must understand all aspects of the origins of the word, and if they are using it, they need to understand that they are publicly pledging their allegiance and real support to any cause that seeks to unjustly target persons of this "culture".

Any black person who has not directly been affected by the physical and mental persecution and horror of slavery and racism during the time in American history where the word nigga held the lethal power of a bullet should not be offended. This word united your ancestors. This word symbolized the power of human nature to survive. This word did not break the resolve of your uprooted culture and this word will not break you either, my nigga.

A WOMAN'S WORTH

The Bible has several examples of how a woman can use her natural power and the results she can command:

Intentional use of Power: Jacob's mother used her female power of persuasion to help him deceive his father; Esther used her beauty and charm to become a queen and save her Jewish culture from genocide; the daughter of Herodias performed a sexual dance for the King who was so aroused by it that he told her she could have up to half of his kingdom; King David was about to kill a man and all the man's sons for disrespecting him but the man's wife stepped in and appeased David and saved her husband's life; God was going to kill Moses until his wife stepped in and did what God had wanted and that act saved Moses' life; and then there was King Solomon who asked God for wisdom over everything and in the end he allowed his wives to lead him astray to the point where he built temples for them to worship foreign gods and idols.

Unintentional use of Power: King David *looked* at a woman and wanted her so bad that he had her husband murdered; Jacob saw a beautiful female and told her dad that he would work for him for free for 7 years if he could marry her...he was tricked and forced to marry her older sister, but he went and told the dad he would *still* work for 7 more years if he could marry the younger sister who he wanted in the beginning; in Genesis it was told that the angels in Heaven *looked* down at the women on Earth and wanted them so badly that they would rather live on Earth and have them than live in Heaven; and finally, David had a son who lusted after his own step-sister so badly that he became physically sick and eventually raped her.

Understanding the worth of a woman and her role in a man's life is crucial, both from the man's point of view and the woman's. On several occasions God warned different men about their selection of a wife because if a wife doesn't love God, she has the power to lead her husband away from God. The first example of this was in the Garden of Eden. The apostle Paul says that sometimes it's best if a man stays single because a married man has a hard time pleasing God because of his strong, natural desire to please his wife. And at the same time, there

At the same time, the Bible mentions how a man should find a good wife because she will complement him and they will both be happy and powerful. In the Garden of Eden, Eve was created because God determined that Adam needed a female companion to complete him.

Here are some Bible verses that talk some more about a woman's worth:

1. Proverbs 11:16 – a kindhearted woman gains honor
2. Genesis 2:24 – a man will leave his parents to be with a woman
3. Proverbs 31:10-31 – a wife of noble character is: worth more than rubies, she has strength and dignity, gives good advice, helps the poor and deserves honor for everything that she does…
4. Proverbs 18:22 - Whoever finds a wife finds something that is good and receives favor from God.
5. Psalm 68:5 – God is a protector of widows

6. Exodus 22:22 – God says He will kill anyone who takes advantage of widows
7. Proverbs 12:24 – a disgraceful wife is like decay in her husband's bones
8. Proverbs 19:13 – a quarrelsome wife is like a constant drip from a leaky roof
9. Proverbs 29:3 – whoever messes with prostitutes will be poor
10. Proverbs 6:26 – an adulterous wife will cost you your life
11. Ecclesiastes 7:26 – thoughts of getting trapped by a woman are worse than contemplating death

In the end, a woman has the support life or death. She needs no weapons of war. Her mind, beauty and natural feminine qualities are her weapons of choice. How a woman follows instructions and where she gets her instructions from determines her worth and value.

CLASH OF THE CULTURES: CUSS/SLANG WORDS

In any relationship, communication seems to be the bonding agent. Couples therapy involves seeking ways to communicate better. Corporations constantly look for the best ways to communicate and reach their target audience. Different cultures communicate within their culture one way and with other cultural groups another way. To be effective in our personal, business and cross-cultural communications, I believe a better understanding of cuss and slang words needs to be discussed.

Purpose of cuss/slang words:

1. In general, these words are words to convey a high level of emotion or passion. It gives your mind a break from all the formality of our language and lets you enter a more creative frame of mind because some things can't always be put into words. Example: You are driving down the highway and a car, not just any car, a new model Lamborghini races by doin' no less than 130mph. If I'm telling you about it and I say "I was driving on the Lodge Freeway heading downtown and I was doing about 90mph; when all of a sudden I hear this loud ass roaring sound and this bright red Lamborghini or some shit blows by like I'm fuckin' standin' still! He had to be doing at least 160 fuckin miles an hour! That shit was crazy!" What should that tell you about my character if anything? What was my excitement/passion level and how could

you tell? What does my choice of words say about my education level? What does my choice of words say about my spirituality?

- You can't really tell much about me as a person by my response. You can't say I'm a bad dad or a good one; that I'm rich or poor.
- You can tell my excitement level was off the charts.
- You can't tell whether or not I graduated high school or if I have a Master's Degree in International Finance.
- You can't even tell if I'm a Christian or not. If someone can show me in the Bible where it says "the use of a particular word to describe the indescribable is a sin"......

2. Cuss/slang words allow the user to give others warnings as to where they are at emotionally. Example: Somebody keeps calling your phone or sending you text and is annoying you. I text back "Leave me the fuck alone!" What should that tell you about my character if anything? What was my excitement/passion level and how could you tell? What does my choice of words say about my education level? What does my choice of words say about my spirituality?

- You can't tell much about my character by my response. You can't say I'm a good dad or a bad one; that I'm rich or poor.
- You can tell my emotions are running hot and on a high level.

- You can't tell my education level by my response.
- You can't even tell if I am a Christian or not. There is nowhere in the Bible that says you have to only use certain words to describe your mood when you're angry. It does say "don't do anything in anger" and I believe that refers to actual actions or regarding the use of language you shouldn't say something in anger that you will regret. To me, letting you know that I've had enough and giving you a verbal warning is fair.

3. Believe it or not, cuss/slang words can be a "term of endearment". What is better for a boss to say to a good employee: "Daryl, I think you are the best employee ever! You are always on time and never complain!! You work lots of overtime when needed and I value you on my team!" or "Hey Daryl, I just wanna let you know that you tha fuckin man around here." What should that tell you about my character if anything? What was my excitement/passion level and how could you tell? What does my choice of words say about my education level? What does my choice of words say about my spirituality?

    - You can't tell anything about my character. You can't say I'm a good dad or a bad one; that I'm rich or poor.
    - You can tell that my praise level for my employee is high and involves so many different aspects that I know I can say what I said and he would know what it is without me going into a drawn out list.

- You can't tell my level of education by my response.
- You can't tell if I am a Christian or not. Nowhere does it say that there are specific words you should use when giving someone praise or acknowledgement.

4. Special case words: nigga, bitch.. In various parts of the world the word "black" is negro, negru or nero. During the period of African American slavery in America, white people called black people Negroes and the slang term became "nigger". Oddly enough, that term has become a widely accepted term of unification among black people. During slavery, the slave families were all separated and sold off to different plantations and it became impossible to say the name of the family who you were related to. The only name/term that all blacks had in common was "nigger". Whether you were light or dark complexion, you were equally treated unequally under the law as a "nigger". It has even become a term used by other cultures to mean "homeboy/close friend". Regarding the word "bitch". I know females who use that term on the regular basis as though it's the female version of nigga. At the same time, a man can call that same female a bitch and a fight will break out. Men even use that term with each other and it could be considered a good or bad thing. What should that tell you about my character if anything? What was my excitement/passion level and how could you tell? What does my choice of words say about my education level? What does my choice of words say about my spirituality?

- You can't tell anything about my character. You can't tell whether I'm a good dad or a bad one; whether I'm rich or poor.
- You can tell my passion level only if you understand the pitch and tone when I use that word.
- You can't tell if I dropped out of school or have a Doctor's Degree in Brain Anatomy.
- You can tell nothing about my spirituality when I use that term

5. Business and cuss/slang words is very tricky because in business dealings you have to be aware of cultural differences regarding politics, word choice and a host of other factors to be able to communicate effectively. Example: I have a brother who has a professional service company. When him and I talk or when he talks to black clients, there is one "language" used; but when a white client comes in, a whole different "language" is used. Depending on who brings what to the table determines the language. I have been around important business meetings where the guy who thought he was in charge was able to cuss but no one else dared; and I have seen meetings where nobody cussed…until certain people walked out the room.
    - You can't tell how sharp a person is in business by whether or not he cusses or uses slang. Is a person who refrains from using cuss/slang words until after the meeting better than a person who uses it during a meeting?
    - You can't tell his pedigree either.

- You can't tell his spirituality either.

Conclusion: The bottom line is that you can't properly judge a person by their use or lack of use, of these words. You are not a better Christian by not using these words. Your segment of a cultural group is no better than another segment of a different cultural group.

Solutions

- Read the situation before you speak.
- Understand that if you use cuss/slang words they may be a barrier to cross cultural communication. At the same time, if you don't use them, that can also be a barrier to communication. In those settings BOTH parties should try and understand the other one's use of the language.
  - Cuss/slang words convey emotions. Emotions can be cultural based and complicated. Once you understand the emotional impact of words, tread softly…or not.

You Got That?

Turn

1. We're getting coked up at a pool hall.
2. I take my turn.
3. When I'm done, I step out the bathroom and one of them goes in to take a turn.
4. I grab a pool stick and take my turn.

(I loved going to pool halls late night and shoot pool and get coked up.)

Mafia Strip Club

5. I'm coked up and don't give a fuck.
6. I'm horny and want to see some strippers.
7. Fuck the mafia!
8. Why can't I touch her?
9. Come closer
10. Turn around

11. Bend over

12. Let me put this $20 in your bikini and touch your ass.

13. I'm coked up and don't give a fuck that this is a mafia-run club!

(I was out East at a Mafia-run strip club getting high. My friend was telling me to chill out. I wasn't worried and didn't care about anything or anybody except the strippers. I just cared about seeing some ass when I was high. We were escorted out by a couple of big ass bouncer-types.)

Bus

14. Alright. Give me $2,000 and I'll make that run right quick.

15. I'll be on the Greyhound, so give me a week.

16. I'm sniffing coke on the bus.

17. Nobody's on the bus but me and the hot chick.

18. I flash my cash.

19. She sits next to me.

20. It's dark. Nobody's looking.

21. We sniff a couple grams of blow.

22. She blows me.

23. I'm on the Greyhound

(I loved running drugs on the bus or train. I usually met some chick who did drugs or at least wanted to trick for some cash.)

Short

24. I know it's short, but that's what I got.

25. The price was higher than I expected.

26. The quality is good though.

27. You straight?

28. Cool.

(I would cop drugs for somebody just so I could take some out their bag for my personal use.)

House Sitting

29. Yeah, I just wanna chill at your house for the weekend.

30. It's nice. It's empty. You're gonna sell it anyways.

31. We good? Cool.

32. "You got that? Here I come."

33. This is a cool ass backyard to get high in!

34. The breeze is a little strong.

35. Hope it don't blow my blow off this plate.

36. I'm almost out.

37. "You got that? Here I come."

(I house sat for people different times. I viewed it as a chance for me to be by myself and get high.)

Baby Sitting

38. Yeah. I'll chill for the weekend and watch your kid.

39. He knows me. We good.

40. "You got that? Here I come."

41. I wanna watch pornos in the bedroom.

42. He wants to watch kid movies in the living room.

43. I'm watching pornos in the bedroom.

44. Last night was a long one.

45. "You got that? Here I come."

46. I lost all my money playing poker!

47. Front me an 8-ball.

48. "You still need that? Here I come."

49. Slow down!

50. Too late!

51. Pull this mutha fucka over!!

52. I have to run back towards the house somehow!

53. "I'm just taking a walk officer".

54. In the back of the police car with another dope case.

55. Aw man! The kid!?!

(I had this incident where my child-watching responsibilities didn't matter…I just wanted to get high. Went to jail this incident.)

Third Shift

56. "Yeah. I'm here by myself all night. You got that? Come through."

57. I don't feel like working anymore.

58. I'll pay you in coke to finish.

59. Open your shirt some more.

60. Stay bent over just like that!

61. "You want some more of that?"

62. Third shift.

(I did a part time night job and just wanted to make sure I called a hot friend of mine that did coke with me so we could get high together and do sex stuff. I didn't care about getting the work done right or not. Got fired.)

Shootin' Craps

63. You don't have any more money?

64. I'll play you for that dope.

65. It's as good as money.

66. What am I gonna do with all this crack?

67. "You want *me* to try that?"

68. No more crack.

(I won all the cash the two guys I was shooting dice with had. One had a bag of crack and wanted to use that as cash. That was my first time seeing it and doing it. I was gonna sell it to make some cash; instead me and two friends rolled corndogs and smoked the whole bag.)

Hot Tub

69. I love hot tubs.

70. "You want me to bring that?"

71. Don't get the fuckin' plate wet!

(Me and this girl went to a friend's house to go hot-tubbing. I didn't care about hot-tubbing: I just wanted to chill and get coked up.)

Night Club

72. I love this club.

73. "You got that?"

74. It's hot in here.

75. Turn the air condition on.

76. "Were there a lot of fine honeys in there?"

(Went to the club many times but most of the time I never made it inside: I was too busy getting high in the car.

Wood Floors

77. I'll sand and stain them for $500.

78. "You got that? Here I come."

79. I'll sand and stain the other floors for $250 just for you.

(I did several contract jobs for cash. Once I got paid, I would get high and to get some more quick cash I would offer to do another job for that person at a discount.)

Cutting Trees

80. "You got that? Here I come."

81. I'll just cut the trees tomorrow.

82. "You still got that?"

83. My chainsaw ain't working.

(If I got paid up front with some drugs, I always had an excuse why I couldn't finish the job so I could keep getting high.)

Parking Lot

84. "Yeah we got that. Here we come."

85. Pull in backwards.

86. Move over there.

87. Pull straight ahead.

88. Is somebody in that car over there?

89. Park over there and just pull straight ahead.

90. We gotta leave.

91. We'll leave in a minute.

(Me and friends would chill in parking lots to get high thinking we had privacy; but we would get too paranoid every time and blow our high.)

Leaky Roof

92. "I'll fix it for that. I gotchoo."

93. I'll finish the rest tomorrow.

94. "You got that? Here I come"

95. My truck ain't starting.

96. I'll be back to finish when I get it running. I gotchoo.

97. "You got that? Here I come."

(Typical situation for me was to get money down from a job, get high and not finish or take the next day off to recover.)

Who is it?

98. "Yeah, I got two of 'em. Here I come."

99. Keep yours on safety.

100. That was crazy!

101.   I told you I gotchoo.

102.   "Let me get some of that."

(I had a guy who I would do "work" for and he would pay me in drugs.)

Casino

103.   I'm on fire tonight!!

104.   "You got that? Here I come."

105.   I need some gas money. "You got that?"

(I loved going to the casino. I would win a bunch of money, blow it all on drugs and strippers and be broke by morning.)

Truck

106.   "You got that? Here I come."

107.   Let me get that then you can use it.

108.   "Where you at? You comin?"

109.   Let me get that then you can use it again.

(I had a very nice pickup truck. I used it a lot as bait for my dope-boy: he could use it for the night or a couple hours if he gave me some drugs.)

It's yours.

110.   "You got that? You comin'?"

111.   If you want it you can get it.

112.   It's brand new.

113.   "You still got that? You comin'?"

(If one of my dope boys liked a piece of jewelry or something I had, I would pawn it or sell it to him for drugs.)

You sure?

114.   "He got that? Here I come."

115.   You were right.

(This one's self explanatory.)

Last Time

116. "You got that? Here I come."

117. Last time.

118. "You still got that? Can *you* come?"

119. Last time.

120. "You still up?"

121. Last time.

122. "I know. You coming?"

123. Last time.

124. "You have reached the voicemail of...."

(I never knew when to stop getting high for the night. I would usually keep going and calling my dope boy until *he* would finally stop answering my calls.)

In addiction, *EVERYTHING* leads to addiction!

Personal Development Plan Notes

Personal Development Plan Notes

Personal Development Plan Notes

Personal Development Plan Notes

Made in the USA
Columbia, SC
26 October 2021